Breaking Scarcity Mindsets and Following a Spiritual Path to Unleashing Abundance

RAY HIGDON

FAITH DRIVEN WEALTH

DISCLAIMER:

The publisher and author have made every reasonable effort to ensure the accuracy and completeness of the information contained in this book at the time of publication. However, they make no representations or warranties, express or implied, as to the accuracy, applicability, fitness, or completeness of the contents. The information provided is for educational and informational purposes only and should not be considered as professional, legal, financial, or business advice.

The author and publisher expressly disclaim any and all liability for any direct, indirect, incidental, or consequential loss or damages whatsoever arising out of or in connection with the use of this book or the application of any information contained herein. This includes but is not limited to, any loss or damage caused by errors, omissions, inaccuracies, or any other cause, regardless of intent or negligence.

By reading and applying the concepts within this book, you acknowledge that you are solely responsible for your actions and outcomes. Success is influenced by numerous factors, including but not limited to individual effort, skill, experience, dedication, and market conditions. No guarantees are made regarding results or earnings.

Scripture quotations marked (ESV) are from the ESV® Bible (The Holy Bible, English Standard Version®), copyright © 2001 by Crossway, a publishing ministry of Good News Publishers. Used by permission. All rights reserved.

Scripture quotations marked (NKJV) are from the New King James Version®. Copyright © 1982 by Thomas Nelson. Used by permission. All rights reserved.

Scripture quotations marked (KJV) are from the King James Version. Public domain.

Scripture quotations marked (NIV) are from the Holy Bible, New International Version®, NIV®. Copyright © 1973, 1978, 1984, 2011 by Biblica, Inc.™ Used by permission. All rights reserved worldwide.

RAY HIGDON

Published by

ISBN 978-1-947814-37-0

Copyright © 2025 by Ray Higdon
All rights reserved.

Except as permitted under the United States Copyright Act of 1976, no part of this publication may be reproduced, distributed, transmitted in any form or by any means, or stored in a data retrieval system, including photocopying, recording, or other electronic or mechanical methods, without the prior written permission of the author.

FAITH DRIVEN WEALTH

"You may say to yourself, 'My power and the strength of my hands have produced this wealth for me.' But remember the Lord your God, for it is he who gives you the ability to produce wealth…"

-Deuteronomy 8:17-18 (NIV)

DEDICATION:

To my Heavenly Father:

Thank You for loving me so much to teach me, mentor me, and guide me. Thank You for never giving up on me and being with me when I didn't see You in the moment. Thank You for making me the way You made me and for all the areas you have blessed me. Thank You for helping me put Your will above my desires!

Love You, Ray

TABLE OF CONTENTS:

Foreword By John Maxwell...		8
Introduction...		11
Chapter 1:	Money Was My Master (But...)	13
Chapter 2:	The Giver of All Good & Perfect Gifts...	18
Chapter 3:	Walk By Faith, Not by Sight...	26
Chapter 4:	What Are the Idols in Your Heart?...	31
Chapter 5:	21 Reasons You Are Broke...	39
Chapter 6:	How I View Wealth...	65
Chapter 7:	God Has an Anointed Brand for You...	71
Chapter 8:	The Ultimate Wealth Hack...	78
Chapter 9:	A Radical Take on Generosity...	83
Chapter 10:	Trusting in God's Plan...	88
Chapter 11:	To Get Wealthy, Do This...	95
Chapter 12:	The Best Type of Freedom...	101
Guest Chapter by Tyler Watson (Nothing Is Impossible)...		107
50 Powerful Prayers...		112
Conclusion...		117
About The Author...		118

FOREWORD by
JOHN C. MAXWELL

One of the most powerful things a leader can do is align their faith and values with their financial goals. This can be challenging because it goes against the natural instinct to store up things for yourself. But what if you could do more, have more, and be more?

I've spent more than five decades studying leadership, and it has become clear to me that one of the greatest indicators of success is a leader's mindset toward resources. Unfortunately, many leaders maintain a scarcity mindset. These are the leaders who are always afraid of using what they have because they think that when they do, they won't have anything left. They build fences around the few valuable items they have and begin to protect them. They keep their hands closed, leaving no room to receive. That's a sad way to live and a bad way to lead.

I agree with my friend, Ray Higdon, that having an abundance mindset is the better way. Leaders with an abundance mindset believe, "There's more than enough. Go and you will find the resources. Your best days are before you." They look at themselves not as a reservoir but as a river. Their goal in life is not to store up or hold up but rather to let go and distribute. Their hands are open as they give, which puts them in a position to receive more.

I'm convinced that learning to maintain an abundance mindset will change the course of your life for the better. I call it the Abundance Paradox: the more you give, the more you have to give—and want to give. What you see, experience, and become is determined by your mindset. Your perspective will control your life today and your potential tomorrow. The good news is you can choose your perspective.

This book isn't just about wealth; it's also about living a life of greater purpose and integrity. One of the first things that grabbed my attention was the subtitle: "Breaking Scarcity Mindsets and Following the Spiritual Path to Unleashing Abundance." What if I told you that it's possible to unleash abundance in your life and that you can have financial freedom? Would that change the way you view your time, your money, and your possessions?

I first met Ray several years ago at a leadership conference, and I noticed right away how passionate he was about helping people. He and I share this passion, so it brought us together immediately. Since then, we've worked together on various projects, and the closer I get to Ray, the more impressed I am by his vision and commitment to faith-driven financial guidance. Ray's drive to help others isn't merely a job—it's a personal mission. He believes deeply in the power of faith to transform lives, especially when it comes to how you leverage your resources.

As you dive into these pages, you'll find this message to be timely and important. I've had many conversations with leaders around the world who revealed their uncertainties about the economy, political systems, and the ever-evolving world of technology, among other questions about the future. Maybe you have some of the same uncertainties or fears about the future. This book will help you see a pathway to abundance that's grounded in faith and integrity. It challenges the common misconceptions about wealth and money that many of us hold and offers a fresh perspective based on biblical principles.

I believe you were created for abundance. Even if you didn't grow up thinking that way, you can step out of the scarcity world and become an abundance person. "Faith Driven Wealth" will help you get there by showing you how to achieve success through aligning your financial goals with your faith. The world is a better place because of people whose perspectives were shaped by abundance thinking—Benjamin Franklin, Alexander Graham Bell, and The Wright Brothers—just to name a few. You can be a part of that group, too.

It's an honor to write the foreword for this transformative book and be one of the first to benefit from its lessons and impact. I encourage you to read and apply its teachings in your own life as well.

- John C. Maxwell

#1 New York Times bestselling author, coach, and speaker often called the country's top leadership authority. He has sold over 24 million books in 50 languages. He is the founder of The John Maxwell Company, The John Maxwell Team, and EQUIP, an organization that has trained over 5 million leaders in 180 countries.

INTRODUCTION

Wealth. Abundance. PROSPERITY.

If there was one topic more controversial to those of *faith*, I don't know what it would be. I believe most Christians have been duped into believing that not only is there virtue in poverty, but they can also ignore every bit of Scripture that talks about loving others *if* someone appears eager to make money.

Then, you have the other extreme. Most people, especially entrepreneurs, base their identity, safety, security, significance, and emotions around how much money they have stored up. They desire to get to a point where they don't have to trust in God because they can trust their Bank of America savings account or their retirement portfolio.

This book *will* help you distinguish what the biblical answer to wealth is: how to think about it, how to multiply and increase it *while* putting God and His Kingdom first!

Why I Titled this Book *Faith Driven Wealth*

Now you may be wondering: if this book is really about abundance, why did I title it *Faith Driven Wealth*? I decided to use wealth because people seem to have an accurate understanding of what *wealth* represents. At the same time, *abundance* is a bit more vague and requires additional explanation. My publishers agreed, so 'wealth' it is.

But notice the subtitle of the book: *Breaking Scarcity Mindsets and Following a Spiritual Path to Unleashing <u>Abundance.</u>*

Wealth without abundance is like having a tree without roots—that could stop producing fruit at any time because without the roots of abundance, there is nothing to sustain it. You could have all the money in the world, but if you're always anxious about whether the tree will keep producing fruit, can you ever be at ease?

I don't think so.

When you live with an abundance mindset, you're not just focused on what you can get—you're also thinking about what you can give, knowing that giving is an important part of the cycle of receiving.

When you truly believe in God's abundance, you start making decisions from a place of confidence and generosity rather than fear and limitation. You need to stop worrying about what you're giving away and start getting excited about the wealth and abundance you can create for yourself *and others.*

1

MONEY WAS MY MASTER (BUT ONLY WHEN I WAS BROKE)

If you are in debt or struggling financially, I understand. I've been there more than once. In 2009, I lost everything in the real estate crash and was in personal foreclosure. I had gone through a divorce, was depressed, a million dollars in debt, and quite honestly felt like a total loser. Sometimes even today, people will come up to me and say, "Ray, you don't understand, I am $30,000 in debt," to which I respond, "Good for you. What restraint you have!"

I had absolutely no clue how to get out of the financial hole I was in. I stressed about money all the time. I thought about it constantly. I would work on *anything* with a hint of a promise to make me money. My emotions were ruled by what was in the bank account.

When I was leaving my house, I always had to look out the front blinds because often there would be a bill collector there to serve me papers, and I definitely wanted to avoid those guys! My late notices and threatening letters would just go on a stack, unopened, until at some point, I would toss the whole pile out. There was nothing I could do anyway, so why bother trying?

One of the most significant ways God blessed me in this season (and He did it before I even knew Him), was by bringing Jessica, my now wife, into my life. She worked at the make-up counter in a department store and eventually started paying my utility bills. I wasn't happy about that at all, but she was young, smart, and beautiful, and believed in me when I didn't.

Fast forward four years to when I had my first million-dollar year, which was in 2013. The year after that, in 2014, I had my first million-dollar month. And the year after that, in 2015, my first million-dollar day became a reality.

What many people don't know is that I'm a bit of a unique entrepreneur in that I've generated over a million dollars in a variety of different lines of business. I've built seven-figure businesses in real estate, network marketing, and affiliate marketing. I've crossed the eight-figure mark, that's over $10 million, in business coaching, selling masterminds, and similar offers from the stage. I've done digital product launches that pulled in anywhere from $750,000 to over $900,000 in less than two weeks.

What's most important to understand is that when I started making millions, money didn't control me, and it wasn't my master.

I have found that many people who are broke think that those with wealth or abundance sit around and think about money all the time. Now, for some, that is true, but for me, once I didn't have to worry about it, I no longer thought much about it. I thought more about impact and helping people with breakthroughs than being overly focused on the bottom line.

Some people think it's the *having* or *not having* money that is the problem. For me, money was only my master when I was broke. It's okay to have money: *just don't let money have YOU.*

Do you fall into either of these camps? Do you get nervous, scared, or anxious when you don't have money, or are you someone who, even after making a lot of money, is only driven by making more? Or are you both?

> *"No one can serve two masters. Either you will hate the one and love the other, or you will be devoted to the one and despise the other. You cannot serve both God and money.*
> **-Matthew 6:24-26 (NIV)**

Let's start with this crucial truth: *Whenever you are afraid and anxious, that's when you trust God the least.* If you are like I used to be, super stressed when the bank account is dry, then it means that you place your trust in money, not God. Instead of, "God is my provider," it's "My money is my provider."

Did you know Scripture tells us that God is responsible for all results? John 3:27 and James 1:17 are just two examples. What if God has recognized your reliance on money *(not Him)* and is trying to help draw you closer to Him?

Now, on the other side, if you have plenty of money, where in your life are you trusting God, or is God no longer needed because you have plenty of money?

> *"Cast but a glance at riches, and they are gone, for they will surely sprout wings and fly off to the sky like an eagle."*
> **-Proverbs 23:5 (NIV)**

Questions and Prayer for Chapter 1...

Questions:

1. Where are you afraid? Challenge yourself to see if that is an area where you don't trust God and His divine power to overcome.
2. Where are you confident? Regarding finances, is it the money you are confident in or your Heavenly Father?

Prayer:

Father, thank You for drawing me closer to You. Thank You for helping me surrender to You. Thank You for helping me to trust and rely on You. God, I thank You for helping me to trust You above money and above the opinions of others. I give You permission to grow me in wisdom and discernment and to help me learn how to put You first, Lord.

(For this and all the prayers going forward, I suggest you say it out loud!)

It's okay to have money: just don't let money have you.

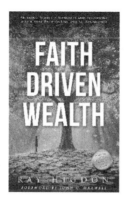

(Take a picture of this page, use #FaithDrivenWealth and post it to your favorite social media sites.)

THE GIVER OF ALL GOOD & PERFECT GIFTS

For most entrepreneurs and business owners, money IS their source. As I mentioned in Chapter One, money, for many, is their source of safety, security, and identity and is deeply connected to their emotions.

I suggest you break that chain. Break away from the spirit of mammon and instead choose to see money as a resource, not *the* source. Jesus calls it out in Matthew 6:24 (KJV) when He says, *'you can't serve both God and mammon.'* When someone is under the 'spirit of mammon,' they obsess over money, have a fear of lack, make decisions based on financial gain, and tie their value to what's in their bank account. "Mammon" is an Aramaic word that essentially means "riches." At its heart, there's an attitude that says: Man doesn't need God—we're self-sufficient. This is what the spirit of mammon tries to tell us: you don't need God. Trust in riches!

Breaking that spirit means shifting our *heart posture*: "I don't serve money, I serve God, and I use money for His purposes." Think of it like this:

Money = Resource
God = <u>SOURCE</u>

God Is <u>THE</u> Source of Unlimited Abundance

God's resources are unlimited. That's right—He doesn't run out, get tired, or hit a limit. Recognizing God as the source of unlimited abundance shifts your mindset. You stop worrying about scarcity and start trusting that God has more than enough to meet your needs and bless others through you. It's easy to think that the economy or your job dictates your financial situation, but God's economy operates differently. He's not bound by the same rules that we have. When you start seeing God as the ultimate source, you realize you're connected to endless possibilities. Financial worry? Let it go. God's got abundance waiting for you—you must trust Him to deliver it in His time and way.

Let Go of Attachments

It's easy to get attached to how you think things should turn out. Whether it's landing that dream job, hitting a financial milestone, or getting that investment to pay off, we often want things to go our way. But releasing attachment to outcomes means letting go of control and trusting God's plan instead.

When you're too focused on one specific outcome, you might miss the bigger blessing God has for you. It's not about giving up on your goals but being flexible and trusting that God knows best. Maybe He's got something even better than what you're aiming for.

So, loosen your grip, stop stressing over every little detail, and trust that God's working things out for your good, even if it doesn't look like what you expected.

Abundance in the Bible

The Bible is filled with examples of God's abundance, both material and spiritual, demonstrating His boundless generosity toward humanity.

- Philippians 4:19 (NIV): *"And my God will meet all your needs according to the riches of his glory in Christ Jesus."*

- 2 Corinthians 9:8 (NIV) highlights God's promise to provide for all our needs through His abundant riches. It reads: *"And God is able to bless you abundantly, so that in all things at all times, having all that you need, you will abound in every good work."* This speaks of God's ability to provide more than enough, equipping us for every good work.

- Psalm 65:11 (NIV) expresses gratitude for God's abundant provision: *"You crown the year with your bounty, and your carts overflow with abundance."*

- Deuteronomy 28:12 (NIV): *"The Lord will open the heavens, the storehouse of His bounty, to send rain on your land in season and to bless all the work of your hands. You will lend to many nations but will borrow from none."* God's blessing on the work of your hands and material abundance is highlighted here.

- And Proverbs 3:9-10 (NIV) which says: *"Honor the Lord with your wealth, with the first fruits of all your crops; then your barns will be filled to overflowing, and your vats will brim over with new wine."*

The "Prosperity Gospel" vs. the "Poverty Gospel"

The prosperity gospel and the poverty gospel represent two opposing theological interpretations within Christianity regarding wealth, material possessions, and God's will for believers. Both approaches tackle the complex relationship between faith and material resources, but they arrive at very different conclusions regarding the role of wealth in a Christian's life.

The Prosperity Gospel

The prosperity gospel promotes the idea that God desires His followers to be prosperous in all areas of life, including health, wealth, and success. It is rooted in passages such as:

- John 10:10 (NIV) which says, *"I have come that they may have life and have it to the full."*

- 3 John 1:2 (KJV) which says, *"I pray that you may prosper in all things and be in health."*

This belief system teaches that faith, positive confession, and generous giving will unlock material blessings and favor from God.

Critics argue that the prosperity gospel encourages followers to give financially in the hope of miraculous returns. It is also criticized for promoting a self-centered faith focused on material gain rather than spiritual growth or service to others.

The Poverty Gospel

The poverty gospel teaches Christians to embrace simplicity, self-denial, and even poverty as a means of spiritual growth and closeness to God. This perspective draws heavily from biblical teachings that warn against the dangers of wealth and advocate for a life of humility and service to the poor, as seen in:

- Matthew 6:19-21 (NIV) which reads, *"Do not store up for yourselves treasures on earth."*
- Matthew 19:24 (NIV) says, *"...it is easier for a camel to go through the eye of a needle than for someone who is rich to enter the kingdom of God."*

Followers of the poverty gospel believe Christians should live humbly and sacrificially rather than amassing personal wealth. In fact, they see wealth as a distraction or a stumbling block in a person's relationship with God. They believe money leads to pride, selfishness, and materialism, which diverts attention from spiritual matters.

Critics of the poverty gospel argue that it can lead to an unhealthy rejection of material resources that could be used for good, such as supporting charitable efforts or improving quality of life. It may also lead to a sense of guilt or shame around success, even when wealth is obtained ethically.

Both the prosperity and poverty gospels draw from Scripture, yet they draw different conclusions.

To be clear, I am a staunch believer that our Heavenly Father wants us to prosper, but not in a selfish, materialistic way. When we place our trust in money rather than God, we risk falling into sin. Jesus warned in Matthew 6:24 (NIV) that *"You cannot serve both God and money."*

From personal experience, let me point out that while you can't serve both God and money, you *can* serve others more effectively *with* money. If we treat money as a resource to be stewarded *wisely*, it can be a powerful force for good. The Bible encourages believers to use their wealth to help the poor, support ministries, and advance God's kingdom.

If your actions don't line up with your values, you're going to feel out of whack and off balance. It's like driving a car that needs an alignment—sure, you can get by, but eventually, things are going to get ugly.

But when your actions are in harmony with your spiritual values, you move through life with a sense of peace and purpose. Any internal tug-of-war between the prosperity gospel and the poverty gospel is precisely that: it's internal.

If you value wealth, accumulate it.

If you value the well-being of others, give generously.

If you value honesty, be transparent in your business dealings.

And if you value simplicity, stop buying things you don't need, and don't flaunt your wealth. Use it humbly and use it well.

Questions and Prayer for Chapter 2...

Questions:

1. Do you see your efforts as the source of your results, or can you start to believe that we are unable to receive unless the Father wills it, as stated in John 3:27?

2. If you lost a big client, contract, or important team member, can you trust that your Heavenly Father has something even better for you?

Prayer:

Father, thank You for breaking off the spirit of mammon from me. I no longer want to live for money; I want to live for YOU. Father, thank You for helping me put Your will above my desires, Lord, as I know "Your ways are higher than my ways" (Isaiah 55:8-9). I thank You in the mighty name of Jesus, Amen.

When your actions are in harmony with your spiritual values, you move through life with a sense of peace and purpose.

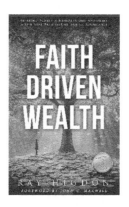

(Take a picture of this page, use #FaithDrivenWealth and post it to your favorite social media sites.)

3

WALK BY FAITH, NOT BY SIGHT

Multiple places in the Bible mention to "walk by faith, not by sight." 2 Corinthians 5:7 (NIV) says. *"For we live by faith, not by sight."*

What does that mean?

I believe it means to walk against your logic and trust God. There have been so many times where God has blessed me by making me uncomfortable moving forward in faith, which totally flew against my logic. In my last book, *The Faith Driven Network Marketer*, I shared several examples of this, but there have been plenty of examples since then.

One Saturday morning, in prayer, I received instructions from the Holy Spirit to take my $10,000 a month salaried salesperson and change them to commission only. What did my logical mind think? *"Oh, this is not going to go well."*

Isn't that what *you* would think?

So, I prayed, *"Lord, do I have to do this today?"* and got a yes! I feared this was going to be a tough thing to do. She had been with me for years. I liked her, and I dreaded this kind of conflict and conversation. Despite all that, I called her and delivered the news.

It didn't go great, but it did go a little better than I thought. Then something amazing happened. One hour later, she called me back and said, "Thank you."

Thank you? I'm like, *come again?* She thanked me because there were a few projects she was genuinely interested in that had nothing to do with me. Still, she didn't feel she could pursue them because of how much I was paying her.

You see, God freed her to pursue the career He wanted for her and the one she also wanted. But my logic, or sight, would *never* have known that.

Here's another example.

My mentor and now friend, Dionne van Zyl, reached out to me one day and said that he felt like the Lord wanted me to help him grow his business. He is in partnership with Graham Cooke, one of the great leaders in the Christian faith, having been teaching for more than 50 years all over the world.

When I prayed about it, I received guidance for turning their app (called Brillant Plus) into a full-blown affiliate/network marketing model. I got exactly what percentages to pay ambassadors, what vendors to use, and exactly how it would work, all in prayer.

I honestly felt weird even pitching it to Dionne the following week. But when I did, he said he loved it. Since we launched, it's going incredibly well! You can check it out at BrilliantMovement.com.

I would never have had that idea, let alone pitch it to Dionne, if I relied on *my* logic. At the time, I felt too busy to take on something like that, but the Lord started freeing up my calendar, and now I believe it will end up being the biggest impact project I have ever taken on.

Questions and Prayers for Chapter 3...

Questions:

1. Think back. Was there ever a time when you were being nudged to do something bold, but it just seemed crazy? Write that book, leave that job, invest in something? What if you started walking in faith, not by logic? (If you can't remember a time, ask God for help.)

2. Are there one or more areas in your life that aren't great that you are accepting, allowing, or tolerating? When I gave God permission to make me excellent in all areas of my life, He helped me lose 30 pounds and grow in every area. He can do that, *and* He wants to do that with you!

Prayer:

Father, thank You for helping me walk more in faith and not just by my own logic. Father, You have my permission to help me become excellent in all areas of my life. Father, thank You for helping me trust You always. I praise You in Jesus' name, Amen.

Father, thank You for helping me walk more in faith and not just by my own logic.

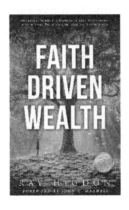

(Take a picture of this page, use #FaithDrivenWealth and post it to your favorite social media sites.)

4

WHAT ARE THE IDOLS IN YOUR HEART?

Ezekiel 14:2-5 (ESV) says: *"And the word of the Lord came to me: Son of man, these men have taken their idols into their hearts, and set the stumbling block of their iniquity before their faces. Should I indeed let myself be consulted by them? Therefore speak to them and say to them, Thus says the Lord God: Any one of the house of Israel who takes his idols into his heart and sets the stumbling block of his iniquity before his face, and yet comes to the prophet, I the Lord will answer him as he comes with the multitude of his idols, that I may lay hold of the hearts of the house of Israel, who are all estranged from me through their idols."*

Understanding the above Scripture was one of the most significant breakthroughs for me in three areas of my life: food, my wife, and money.

For the purposes of this book about faith driven wealth, I will share my breakthroughs regarding my wife and money as they *do* relate, and I believe many struggle with similar obstacles.

I accepted Christ in November of 2022 and share the full story in my book *The Faith Driven Network Marketer* and also on YouTube (you can watch at HigdonGroup.com/apology).

The way that God wired me (that I cannot boast about) is that He made me relentless. I am a dog-with-a-bone kind of guy. Either I am 'all-in' in complete obsession, or I want absolutely nothing to do with whatever topic.

My first week with Christ, I hired a Hebrew/Aramaic mentor, and I became obsessed with learning the Word. I remember seeing an interview with David Green, the founder of Hobby Lobby, where he said, "My life changed when I turned every major and minor decision over to prayer and the Lord."

I thought, well, heck, if that is possible, I will do that too! (I spent a bit of time with David at his headquarters in Oklahoma, which I'll share more about later.)

My Obsession with Hearing from God

I became obsessed with hearing from God and started constantly asking Him questions. Asking for answers, by the way, is biblical. James 1:5 (NKJV): *"If any of you lacks wisdom, let him ask of God, who gives to all liberally and without reproach, and it will be given to him."*

So, I would take note of the instructions I would receive and was obedient even when the instructions seemed crazy. Now, for those who don't believe you can hear from God, I want to help you, as *this is* the most valuable thing that I have *ever* learned. When I hear God, or perhaps more technically from the Holy Spirit, it is <u>not</u> some Charlton Heston or James Earl Jones in

King James voice—it is instead my own inner voice but just in words I would not use. At the end of this chapter, I will share a prayer for you to test to see what you get.

As I started consistently getting answers in prayer, there was a problem. I started noticing that there were three areas where I consistently received answers that seemed off or misguided. (Many of the answers I would later confirm were not answers from God but from my own emotional state.)

Once I discovered the verse from Ezekiel, I prayed to see if there were idols in my heart, and there were. Idols in your heart mean anything you secretly put above God in your desires, trust, or priorities.

I had emotional attachments around food, money, and not letting my wife Jessica down. It's very important when praying to seek His will and avoid having an emotional attachment to what *you hope* He says! Because I was placing such importance on those topics, I was not getting accurate wisdom from Him.

I recall one day, Jessica and I were arguing. We were, yet again, arguing about, guess what? Money! You see, she had grown up with a mother (who has since passed) who had a lot of money, then later lost it all. As a result, Jess had a fear of losing money and having to rely on others, as she saw her Mom experience.

You take that issue, plus my desire to never let her down, and it has led to quite a few challenging conversations over the years.

This time, I led the conversation differently, and I felt it. Afterward, I felt the need to pray about it, and I received in prayer: *"I had to get you to trust Me more than you were worried about letting her down."*

Wow.

Emotional Attachment to Money

If you have fears or past wounds around money, you may likely have a more emotional attachment (an idol of the heart) to money than wanting to hear God's will. Here are several examples of money wounds that I have coached people through:

1. If you had parents who made a lot of money and then lost it, it's very likely you have an unconscious belief that if you also make a lot of money, you too will lose it, so you may sabotage ever making a lot of money.

2. I see this in a lot of children of immigrant parents. If you had parents who worked really hard but never made much money, you may feel you aren't worthy of an easy life and will sabotage it.

3. If your parents or one parent was obsessed with success and ignored you, you may sabotage success as you don't want anyone to feel the way you felt.

Additionally, I hear people talk themselves out of investing in themselves, avoid starting that business, and never find the time or resources to help them write that book.

Divine permission should lead to bold action.

There have been many times when the Lord called me to give more money than I wanted in a donation or an investment. Instead of justifying why I shouldn't, I just trusted Him.

I love this saying from my friend Graham Cooke: *"God isn't trying to talk you out of something; He's trying to talk you*

INTO something." This is powerfully said in 2 Corinthians 5:17 (NIV):

> *"Therefore, if anyone is in Christ, the new creation has come: The old has gone, the new is here!"*

Too many of us either look at what we have accumulated and want to protect it, or we focus on the mistakes we have made in the past, versus the power of God to radically transform all our circumstances.

Having Trouble Hearing Him?

There are six things that I have found in my relentless pursuit to hear from God that can block or limit you from hearing Him:

1. Your language. Proverbs 18:21 (NIV): *"The tongue has the power of life and death..."* If you keep saying you never hear from Him, you *will* limit hearing from Him.

2. If you are not honoring Him. Isiah 59:1-2 (NIV) explains this clearly: *"But your iniquities have separated you from your God; your sins have hidden his face from you, so that he will not hear."* There have been times when I did not honor Him and had to ask for forgiveness to get back to hearing from Him.

3. Idols of the heart.

4. Your own will. You have already made up your mind about what you are going to do and aren't seeking His will in the matter.

5. Spiritual Warfare (yes, there is such a thing). This book won't get into much of this, but it is real, and I have absolutely received wrong answers that didn't come from me or God.

6. Your emotions. If you are overly emotional about what you are asking God, overly afraid, overly anxious, overly addicted to the outcome you are hoping for, it could hamper you hearing from Him.

Questions and Prayers for Chapter 4...

Questions:

1. To hear from God, get yourself in a surrendered state. (For me, a surrendered state is on my knees, clear of distractions, and *not* rushed or in a hurry.) Grab a pen and paper and ask this question in prayer: Father, how do You see me? (Remember: His voice is not Darth Vader; it's your own inner voice, but words you would not likely say.)

2. In that same surrendered state, ask: Father, if I have any idols in my heart, please reveal them to me and make them clear. What came up for you?

Prayer:

Father, thank You for telling me how You see me, and Father, thank You for revealing to me any idols of my heart. I thank You for removing all idols from my heart so I can clearly hear You moving forward, and I thank You for putting Your will above my emotions and desires. I also thank You for helping me delight in being obedient to You! I thank You in the mighty name of Jesus Christ, Amen!

If you have fears or past wounds around money, it's likely you may have a more emotional attachment (an idol of the heart) to money than wanting to hear God's will.

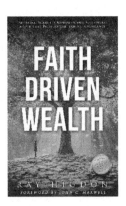

(Take a picture of this page, use #FaithDrivenWealth and post it to your favorite social media sites.)

5

21 REASONS YOU ARE BROKE

Our minds are powerful. What we believe shapes our reality. When it comes to attracting wealth, one of the biggest obstacles is our own limiting beliefs. These are the thoughts and assumptions that we've picked up over time, often without even realizing it. They sneak into our minds and start controlling our actions, making it tough to achieve the prosperity we're capable of.

If you're holding onto the idea that *money is evil* or that you're *not worthy of success*, it's time to finally let those thoughts go.

God created a world of abundance, not scarcity. And when you believe that there's not enough to go around, you're living in a mindset of scarcity and lack, and that's a major block to attracting wealth. Instead, embrace the truth that God's blessings are infinite.

The Top 21 Limiting Beliefs

This entire book could be filled with nothing but these limiting beliefs, but I disciplined myself by limiting the list to what I consider to be the 21 most prevalent and negatively impactful on our lives.

☐ Limiting Belief #1: Money is the Root of All Evil

It should be no surprise that the belief that "money is the root of all evil" tops the list. Many people feel conflicted about having money as if being wealthy is something to apologize for. This common misconception comes from misquoting 1 Timothy 6:10. What 1 Timothy 6:10 (KJV) *actually* says is: *"The love of money is the root of all evil."*

Hebrews 13:5 (NIV) advises: Keep your lives free from the love of money and be content with what you have because God has said, *"Never will I leave you; never will I forsake you."* Regular reflection on what truly matters in life—faith, family, friendships—helps shift the focus away from acquiring more possessions.

The Bible is full of stories of God blessing His people with wealth, not to weigh them down but to uplift them and enable them to do great things.

Consider the story of Abraham:

God promised to make him the father of many nations and blessed him with great wealth (Genesis 13:2). Abraham's wealth wasn't a burden; it was a testament to God's faithfulness and a means to fulfill His promise. Similarly, Job, after enduring immense suffering, was blessed with even greater wealth than he had before (Job 42:10). These examples show that wealth is not a curse or a burden but a blessing from God.

So, answer this question: If God blesses us with wealth, how can money be the root of all evil? It doesn't make any sense.

However, with great blessing comes great responsibility. Luke 12:48 (KJV) tells us: *"For unto whomsoever much is given, of him shall be much required."*

This means that, while wealth is a blessing, it also comes with the responsibility to use it wisely and in ways that honor God. It's not about accumulating wealth for its own sake but about using it to bless others and advance God's kingdom.

When you view wealth as a blessing, you can approach it with gratitude and joy rather than guilt or fear. You recognize that your wealth is a gift from God, and you're motivated to use it in ways that reflect His goodness and love. This mindset allows you to enjoy your wealth without being weighed down, knowing that you're fulfilling God's purpose for your life.

Money itself is not inherently evil. It is a neutral resource. A tool. And like any tool, money can be used for good or for harm, depending on the intentions of the heart. It is the *love* of money—the obsession with wealth, greed, and materialism—that leads people away from God's will.

The idea that God wants you to be poor is one of the biggest misconceptions out there, so let's clear this up once and for all. God does not desire poverty for any of His children.

Throughout the Bible, we see examples of God blessing people with wealth, not to mention promises of prosperity for those who follow His ways.

Poverty isn't a virtue. And it certainly isn't God's will for you. Consider Jeremiah 29:11 (NIV), where God says, *"For I know the plans I have for you... plans to prosper you and not to harm you, plans to give you hope and a future."* Does that sound like a God who wants you to struggle financially? Well, does it?

God's plans for us include abundance, not lack.

So why do so many people think that God wants them to be poor? I think a lot of this comes from a misunderstanding of the Scriptures and the teachings of Jesus.

Yes, Jesus taught about the dangers of loving money more than God, but He also taught about *using wealth responsibly.* For example, in the parable of the talents (Matthew 25:14-30), the servants who wisely invested and grew their master's money were praised, while the one who did nothing with it was reprimanded. This story isn't just about money; it's about using the resources God gives us to their fullest potential.

When you think about wealth in the context of your faith, remember that God's blessings come with responsibility. It's not about hoarding wealth or becoming obsessed with money—it's using what God gives you to bless others and advance His kingdom. Poverty may be a reality for many, but it's not God's desire for you. He wants you to thrive and live a life that reflects His abundance.

We need to flip the script on how we view wealth. Too often, wealth is painted as something negative, something that corrupts and leads people astray. But here's the truth: wealth, in and of itself, is neutral. It's neither good nor evil. It's how we use it that makes the difference.

When we see wealth as an instrument for good, we can harness it to make a positive impact on the world around us.

The Bible gives us plenty of examples of wealth being used for good. Look at King Solomon, one of the wealthiest men in the history of God's creation, who used his riches to build the temple in Jerusalem, a place where people could worship God. Or consider Joseph of Arimathea, a wealthy man who used his resources to provide a tomb for Jesus. These men didn't see their wealth as something to be ashamed of; they saw it as a tool to fulfill God's purposes.

1 Timothy 6:17-19 (NIV) advises, *"Command those who are rich in this present world not to be arrogant nor to put their hope in wealth, which is so uncertain, but to put their hope in God... Command them to do good, to be rich in good deeds, and to be generous and willing to share."* This passage doesn't condemn wealth; it calls us to use it wisely and generously.

Ultimately, wealth gives you the power to make a difference, to fund ministries, to help the needy, and to create opportunities for others. When you view wealth as a tool for good, you're aligning your financial success with God's plan. Instead of fearing wealth or feeling guilty about it, embrace it as a blessing from God and use it to further His kingdom. Remember, it's not about how much you have, but what you do with what you have that counts.

Ecclesiastes 9:16 (NIV) says, *"Wisdom is better than strength, but the poor man's wisdom is despised. His words are not heard."*

Interesting.

This may fly in the face of some people who have bought into this incorrect doctrine that being broke is virtuous.

Have you been sold the concept of the poverty gospel? You rebelled so much against the prosperity gospel that you're embracing the poverty gospel of being meek and broke with no money at all, thinking this makes you virtuous.

☐ Limiting Belief #2. I Don't Deserve to Be Wealthy

The second on my list of limiting beliefs is the belief that you don't deserve to be wealthy, which is rooted in feelings of inadequacy or unworthiness. But the Bible reminds us that God's blessings, including wealth, are not based on our merit but on His grace and love.

Feeling unworthy of wealth often stems from a lack of understanding God's nature. God is a generous Father who delights in blessing His children. In Matthew 7:11 (NIV), Jesus says, *"If you then, though you are evil, know how to give good gifts to your children, how much more will your Father in heaven give good gifts to those who ask him!"*

God does not want us to live in poverty or to feel undeserving of His blessings. Instead, He wants us to live in the fullness of His provision.

Do You Believe You Are Worthy of Wealth?

Do you feel guilty over past wrongdoings? Over moral failures? Or that you don't pray or attend church often enough? Do you see others as being more deserving? If you perceive others as being more righteous or deserving, you end up feeling inadequate and unworthy by comparison. This leads to a subconscious belief that you are somehow *disqualified* from receiving wealth or material blessings.

This is especially true for people who have lived in poverty for a long time. They might internalize the belief they're meant to stay poor as if their poverty has been a sign of God's will.

This isn't how God works.

Wealth is not intended just for your personal gain—it is also for God's purposes. God blesses you so that you can be a blessing to others.

Deuteronomy 8:18 (NIV) reminds us, *"But remember the Lord your God, for it is He who gives you the ability to produce wealth…"* God wants you to prosper, but you've got to believe it's possible.

☐ Limiting Belief #3: Success Is for Other People, Not Me

Why wouldn't it be for you, too? The Bible teaches us that God has a plan and purpose for *each* of His children. In Jeremiah 29:11 (NIV), God declares, *"For I know the plans I have for you, plans to prosper you and not to harm you, plans to give you hope and a future."* God's plans include success and prosperity for *all* who trust in Him.

God does not play favorites. Acts 10:34 (NIV) says, *"…God does not show favoritism."* If God has blessed others with success, He can do the same for you. Instead of believing success is for someone else, maybe it's time to step out in faith.

☐ Limiting Belief #4: I'm Not Smart Enough for Wealth

The Bible tells us that God equips those He calls. For example, in Exodus 4:10-12 (NIV), Moses expressed his insecurity about speaking to the Pharaoh, but God reassured him: *"Now go; I will help you speak and will teach you what to say."* God does not call the qualified; *He qualifies the called.*

Success and wealth are not dependent on your abilities but on God's strength working through you. God often uses those who feel inadequate or unqualified to accomplish great things for His kingdom. It's not always just about you.

When we see wealth as an instrument for good, we can harness it to make a positive impact on the world.

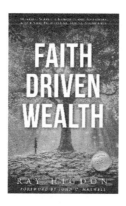

(Take a picture of this page, use #FaithDrivenWealth and post it to your favorite social media sites.)

☐ Limiting Belief #5: Rich People Are Greedy or Selfish

Many people, when they see a rich person, assume they got their money through luck, inheritance, or illegal means. Regardless of how a person obtained their wealth, the Bible shows that wealth does not corrupt a person. It is the condition of the *heart* that matters.

Some of the greatest figures in Scripture were wealthy, yet they were faithful and generous stewards of their riches. Abraham, Job, and King Solomon were incredibly wealthy but are remembered for their faith and obedience to God.

1 Timothy 6:17 (NIV) says, *"Command those who are rich in this present world not to be arrogant nor to put their hope in wealth, which is so uncertain, but to put their hope in God..."* The issue is not wealth but how one uses it. Wealth can be used for selfish gain or for advancing God's kingdom by helping the poor, funding missions, and supporting the church.

In Luke 12:48 (NIV), Jesus teaches, *"From everyone who has been given much, much will be demanded..."* Wealth is not free. With wealth comes responsibility.

☐ Limiting Belief #6: You Can't Be Wealthy and Have a Balanced Life

What? You might assume that accumulating wealth will require sacrificing important aspects of your life—be it family, health, spiritual well-being, or something else. The Bible teaches that God desires us to live abundant *and balanced* lives. In John 10:10, Jesus says, *"I have come that they may have life, and have it to the full."* Fullness means every aspect of our lives—spiritual, emotional, relational, and financial.

A balanced life is about keeping God at the center of everything we do. Matthew 6:33 says, *"But seek first His kingdom and His righteousness, and all these things will be given to you as well."* When we prioritize our spiritual lives and trust God to provide for us, we *can* experience both wealth and balance. It is only when we allow the pursuit of wealth to become an obsessive priority that our lives get out of balance.

☐ Limiting Belief #7: You Need Money to Make Money

The belief that you need money to make money is a sign of a scarcity mindset. The Bible teaches that God provides for His people, even from the humblest beginnings. In the parable of the mustard seed (Matthew 13:31-32), Jesus describes how something as small as a mustard seed can grow into a large tree, symbolizing how God can take even the smallest resources and multiply them for His purposes.

You've probably heard the phrase *"rags to riches,"* right? Wealth is not dependent on the amount of money you start with but on God's blessing and our faithfulness. The widow's offering in Mark 12:41-44 is a powerful example. Jesus praised her for giving a small amount because it was all she had, showing that God values the *heart* behind our actions more than the amount of wealth we possess. Ultimately, it is God's blessing, not the size of your bank account, that determines your financial success.

☐ Limiting Belief #8: If I Fail, People Will Judge Me

This belief is clearly rooted in fear and shame. However, from a biblical perspective, failure is not the end but often a stepping stone toward a greater purpose. The Bible is filled with examples of people who failed but were still used mightily by God.

Peter, one of Jesus' closest disciples, denied Christ three times, yet Jesus forgave him and commissioned him to lead the early church (John 21:15-17). His failure did not define him; rather, it was part of his journey toward becoming a leader of the faith.

Okay, let's say you try and fail. So what? Try again. When we view failure through the lens of faith, we see it as a temporary setback, not a permanent label.

Proverbs 24:16 (NIV) reminds us: *"For though the righteous fall seven times, they rise again..."* This verse emphasizes the need for resilience in the face of failure. Fact: God does not expect perfection from us, but He does expect us to trust in His grace and mercy when we fall.

Romans 8:28 (NIV) assures us that *"...in all things God works for the good of those who love Him..."* Even in our failures, God is working for our good. God's grace is sufficient, and He can turn even our failures into something beautiful if we remain faithful and trust in His plan.

☐ Limiting Belief #9: It's Too Late for Me to Succeed

This belief is yet another lie we tell ourselves—and trust me, the devil loves it. The Bible shows us that God's timing is perfect, and it is never too late for Him to accomplish His purposes in our lives.

Joel 2:25 (KJV) God declares: *"I will restore to you the years that the locust hath eaten..."* This verse tells us that God can redeem time and opportunities that we feel have been lost. No matter how long it takes, God can still bring about His plans for our success if we remain faithful and trust in His timing.

Moses was 80 years old when God called him to lead the Israelites out of Egypt (Exodus 7:7). His most significant achievements came later in life, proving that age or past circumstances do not limit God's ability to work through us. God can bring about success at any stage of life. As long as we are alive and willing, it is never too late to fulfill the calling and purpose God has for us.

Side note: In Genesis 17:15-17, God promised Abraham and Sarah a child in their old age. Abraham was 100 when he became the father of Isaac, fulfilling God's promise and proving that it is never too late for God to bring success and blessing. How's that for it never being too late?

☐ Limiting Belief #10: I'm Not Lucky Enough to Be Rich

Wealth is not a matter of luck, chance, or fate. Yes, someone can win millions in the lottery, but why would you assume it was anything other than God's work?

Not luck. Not chance. Not fate.

Him.

While the world may see wealth as something that happens randomly, believers understand that God is in control of all things and that His plans for us are good.

☐ Limiting Belief #11: I'd Have to Overcharge People to Get Rich

This belief can be a wealth killer, especially for:

- Business owners who set the price for the products or services they offer.
- Writers, contractors, graphic designers, website developers, or other freelance workers who set their rates.
- Artists, painters, sculptors, and illustrators who set their own prices.
- Independent life coaches and fitness trainers who set the pricing structures for what they offer.

Have you ever hired a band to play at a wedding? I have. The prices they quote are wildly different. If you get ten quotes, you'll get everything from $200 to $20,000 for a four-hour gig. Can the $20,000 band really be 100 times better than the lower-priced band? No. What they have is a belief in their own value. (The same is true for wedding photographers.)

I remember the first time I quoted $20,000 to deliver a keynote presentation at a conference. I wondered: Who was I to charge that much? Is charging that fee fair to them? The bigger question is, is asking for less fair to me?

Our work is an act of worship and service to God. Charging appropriately is a way of honoring the gifts and opportunities He has entrusted to us.

☐ Limiting Belief #12: I'd Have to Work Too Hard to Get Rich

Striving to exhaustion is what many people associate with gaining wealth. And, yes, God calls us to work diligently and with integrity, as Proverbs 12:11 (NIV) says: *"Those who work their land will have abundant food, but those who chase fantasies have no sense."*

But the idea that you must work extremely hard to make money is just flat-out wrong. In fact, the opposite is often true. In many cases, the harder someone works often has the opposite effect. Take a construction worker, for example. They are paid a wage in exchange for their time and labor. However, there are limits to the amount of time and effort they have to offer.

I have come to understand that God invites us to work from a place of rest and trust in Him. In Matthew 11:28-30 (NIV), Jesus says, *"Come to me, all you who are weary and burdened, and I will give you rest."*

☐ Limiting Belief #13: There's Not Enough Money to Go Around

The belief that "there's not enough money to go around" reflects a scarcity mindset, which is contrary to the biblical truth of God's abundant provision. In Philippians 4:19 (NIV), Paul says, *"And my God will meet all your needs according to the riches of His glory in Christ Jesus."* God's resources are infinite, and He promises to provide for the needs of His people. Believing in scarcity limits our faith in God's ability to bless us abundantly and is actually an insult to God's power.

Psalm 24:1 (NIV) says, *"The earth is the Lord's, and everything in it..."* All resources belong to God, and He is not limited by the world's economy.

Trust me, there is plenty.

God isn't stingy with His blessings.

RAY HIGDON

Wealth is not a matter of luck, chance, or fate. Yes, someone can win millions in the lottery, but why would you assume it was anything other than God's work? Not luck. Not chance. Not fate. Him.

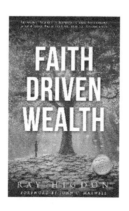

(Take a picture of this page, use #FaithDrivenWealth and post it to your favorite social media sites.)

☐ Limiting Belief #14: I'm Not from a Rich Family

This belief suggests wealth is inherited or tied to an individual's background. But the Bible shows us that God's blessings are *not* determined by family lineage or social status but by His grace and provision.

God is not limited by our background or circumstances.

Many of the great leaders in the Bible came from humble beginnings. Joseph was sold into slavery by his brothers, yet God raised him to be second-in-command in Egypt. David was a shepherd boy, the youngest in his family, yet he became the king of Israel. God can elevate anyone, regardless of their background, to positions of wealth and influence and blessing.

In 1 Samuel 16:7 (NIV), God reminds Samuel, *"The Lord does not look at the things people look at. People look at the outward appearance, but the Lord looks at the heart."*

There's that word *heart* again.

Wealth is not something that must be inherited from earthly parents but a blessing that comes from our Heavenly Father. When we align our lives with God's principles and trust in His provision, we are not limited by our family history. God can and will bless those who faithfully serve Him, regardless of their background.

☐ Limiting Belief #15: If I'm Rich, People Won't Like Me

The belief that if you become wealthy, people won't like you stems from the fear of rejection. However, Scripture teaches us that our worth and identity are found in Christ, not in the opinions of others. Galatians 1:10 (NIV) says, *"Am I now trying to win the approval of human beings, or of God? Or am I trying to please people? If I were still trying to please people, I would not be a servant of Christ."*

Our primary goal should be to please God, not to worry about the approval of others.

Yes, not everyone will understand or appreciate your success. In fact, they may dislike you because of it. There's plenty of jealousy to go around. But this should <u>not</u> deter you. Remember: Jesus Himself was rejected by many despite His perfect life and mission.

As long as you remain humble and give glory to God for your success, you can trust that He will surround you with the right people who will support and encourage you on your journey.

☐ Limiting Belief #16: My Financial Situation Will Never Change

Believing that your financial situation is unchangeable often stems from a defeatist mindset. It can happen from growing up in an environment where helplessness was the norm. This belief can also take root through constant criticism or a lack of encouragement, making a person assume that financial progress is out of reach.

But the Bible teaches us that with God, all things are possible. In Philippians 4:13 (KJV), Paul declares, *"I can do all things through Christ who strengthens me."* This includes overcoming financial challenges and breaking free from a cycle of poverty. God is a God of transformation, and He can change any situation when we place our trust in Him.

Throughout Scripture, we see examples of God providing for His people in miraculous ways. In 2 Kings 4:1-7, a widow was facing financial ruin, but through the prophet Elisha, God provided an abundance of oil that she was able to sell to pay off her debts and live on. This story shows that even in the direst financial situations, God can provide a way out. With faith and perseverance, no situation is beyond God's ability to transform.

☐ **Limiting Belief #17: I'm Too Young to be Successful**

When someone believes they are too young to be successful, they haven't paid attention to reality.

- Mozart began composing music at age five and was famous by his teens.
- Joan of Arc became a French military leader at 17.
- Mark Zuckerberg was 19 when he started Facebook, and Bill Gates was only 20 when he founded Microsoft.
- A kid named Evan Moana started a YouTube channel while he was in the fourth grade and became a millionaire reviewing kids' toys.
- Moziah Bridges, who was featured a few years ago on *Shark Tank,* started a company selling bow ties at age nine.

And have you ever heard of *Me & the Bees Lemonade,* which is sold at Costco? It was started by a young girl named Mikaila Ulmer, who launched her company... *at the age of four.*

Oh, I know what you're thinking: these kids didn't do it alone. They probably had help from their parents. I'm not lucky enough to have anyone jump in and help me. I don't have the right connections.

Oh, really.

What about God?

Well, whose fault is it that you are not connected to God? It's not God's fault. That's on you.

Scripture teaches that God uses people of all ages for His purposes. In 1 Timothy 4:12 (NIV), Paul encourages the young Timothy, *"Don't let anyone look down on you because you are young, but set an example for the believers in speech, in conduct, in love, in faith and in purity."* Age is not a barrier to success when God's hand is upon your life.

☐ Limiting Belief #18: I'm Too Old to Be Successful

Okay, what about the other end of the age spectrum? Psalm 92:14 (NIV) says, *"They will still bear fruit in old age, they will stay fresh and green."* For example:

- Harland Sanders franchised his first KFC at the age of 62.
- Ray Kroc was 52 when he turned McDonald's into a fast-food empire.
- Henry Ford didn't create the Model T until he was 45, after years of failed businesses and setbacks.
- Vera Wang started her fashion design career at 40, after working as a journalist and a figure skater.

- Laura Ingalls Wilder wrote her book (later renamed Little House on the Prairie for TV) and got it published at the age of 65.

- Anna Mary Robertson Moses (aka, Grandma Moses) didn't start her career as an artist until she was almost 80, which is interesting because Moses (from the Bible) was 80 years old when he was called to lead the Israelites out of Egypt.

Whether young or old, God has a plan for each season of our lives. When we trust in His timing and purpose, we can achieve success regardless of our age. God's power is not limited by human timelines. He is able to use anyone who is willing, no matter how young or old.

☐ Limiting Belief #19: Taking Risks Can Ruin Your Life

The belief that "taking risks will ruin your life" stems from a fear of failure and uncertainty. But you know what? Having faith itself is a risk—trusting in something we cannot see. Hebrews 11:1 (ESV) defines faith as *"the assurance of things hoped for, the conviction of things not seen."* The Bible encourages us to step out in faith, trusting that God will guide and protect us, even when the outcome is uncertain.

In Matthew 14:29-31, Peter took the risk of stepping out of the boat and walking on water toward Jesus. Although he faltered, Jesus was there to catch him. In moments of doubt, God is always there to lift us up. Playing it safe may *seem* secure, but it often keeps us from experiencing the fullness of what God has for us.

To be clear, taking risks doesn't mean being reckless. It means trusting God's direction rather than relying solely on your own calculations. When we step out in faith, trusting in God's guidance, we can be confident that He will direct our steps and protect us.

Wealth does not corrupt a person. It is the condition of the heart that matters.

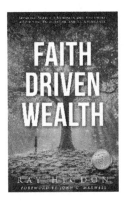

(Take a picture of this page, use #FaithDrivenWealth and post it to your favorite social media sites.)

☐ Limiting Belief #20: Being Rich Will Make Me a Bad Person

Boy, this is a big one. It goes right back to the idea that money is the root of all evil.

The belief that being rich will make you a bad person or will automatically lead to greed or moral compromise isn't very rational. Again (as stated earlier), wealth is not the problem; it is the *obsession with wealth* that can lead us to sin.

Many godly individuals in the Bible were wealthy and used their resources for good. Job, for instance, was a rich man who remained righteous and faithful to God. And do you know what? When Job lost everything, God restored his wealth and blessed him even more abundantly (Job 42:10-12).

☐ Limiting Belief #21: I'll Just Lose it Like "____" Did

This is actually very common. If you watched your parents (or someone who influenced you as a kid) have or make a bunch of money and then lose it, it is very likely you created a program that is stored in your subconscious that has you believe that if you make a bunch of money, you too will lose it.

Our mind works to protect us from bad memories and experiences. I have found that every single person—100% of the people who want to be consistent in their business but are not—are *all* due to wounds from their childhood and observations they made as kids.

You *can* get over this, though. I have coached quite a few people through this, as I have all the other beliefs.

Questions and Prayers for Chapter 5...

Questions:

1. Which of the 21 Limiting Beliefs resonated with you? Write them down. Be aware of them. You can't change anything you aren't aware of first, and we will use these in the prayer.
2. Who would you feel bad for if you reached all your goals? This is an incredible exercise if you choose to do it. Imagine you have all your monetary goals. Would your best friend, siblings, parents, or anyone else important to you be hurt or jealous? This may be what has you sabotaging your success.

Prayer:

(Make a list of the beliefs from this chapter that you resonated with, and go to the Father for His help using the following prayer):

Father, thank You for helping me be better with _____. Father, I give You permission to remove _____ from my heart, mind, and life. Father, thank You for healing all parts of me. Thank You for healing my conscious and subconscious to better receive Your blessings and Your favor. Father, thank You for helping me believe I deserve all of Your gifts! I thank You in the mighty, matchless name of Jesus Christ!

6

HOW I VIEW WEALTH

I've had interesting experiences with wealth. Twice in my life, I have been under heavy debt, over a million dollars each time and then I've also been blessed to accrue millions more.

As mentioned in a previous chapter, money was only my master when I was broke, as it became my all-encompassing thought and worry. When I started making plenty of money, it truly became an afterthought, making an impact and significance became my master.

The person who really rattled my cage about how I viewed wealth was David Green, founder of Hobby Lobby, who I mentioned earlier. As a kid, he dreamed of being a dime store manager, and that would have made him the most successful guy in his family! He and his wife started Hobby Lobby, which, at the time of this writing, has 44,000 employees, 1,055 stores, and revenue of over eight billion dollars a year.

Many years ago, David Green started donating 50% of all profits to charity. Although Hobby Lobby is not a public company, and this is not verified, the rumor is that he gave over $750 million to charity last year. Not bad.

I highly encourage you to read his book, *"Leadership Not By The Book,"* and watch his interviews on YouTube. It's incredible how someone who has access to so much money views his wealth. He sees his success, wealth, and life as God's property, and he stewards them accordingly. In one interview, a reporter asked him if he was making enough money after the company crossed one billion in revenue after the company announced it would be opening another 300 stores. He replied, *"It will never be enough as each store that opens is an opportunity for more people to come to Christ."*

Wow.

I had the chance to meet and spend a little bit of time with David. He was as humble as can be, and he really enjoyed me sharing the story of bringing my mom to Christ, as he has such a deep love for his mother as well. The day after I met him, I also brought my Dad to Christ.

So how does it work?

I pray on every dollar I spend, invest, give, etc. I see the money and resources that God has given me in life as things to be stewarded, not just spent however I want. I know this sounds extreme, but I don't spend a dime unless I receive that it's a good idea from Him.

Some people who read this may wonder if I spend some crazy amount of time in prayer, stumbling around indecisively. The truth is, I have built the muscle to hear from Him frequently, so answers come quickly, and His wisdom puts me at ease so that I can make the best decision for myself, my family, and our future.

I suspect that money is the biggest stumbling block for Christians, and that's why I believe this book and the topic of money are so important.

Over and over, I see people stay stuck in their lives because they are holding onto their money due to fear. Many times, God has nudged me to invest in myself instead of basing my trust on the money I am holding onto.

God has also prevented me from making some dumb investments, so don't get me wrong. We aren't to be frivolous with money; we are to use this resource purposefully. His ways are higher than our ways, so He knows when, where, and with whom your money is best invested.

Earlier in this book, I mentioned idols of the heart. I believe money is likely the most common form of an idol in your heart, so when you pray about anything connected to money, you must let your emotions go and not be addicted to whatever answer He is going to give you.

He Grew Me in Peace and Patience

Here's a fun story about how God grew me in peace and patience around money. Not that long ago, I transferred two large amounts of money from investment accounts to my bank account. I was told I would have it by Friday or Monday at the latest.

Friday comes, and nothing. Monday, Tuesday, and Wednesday pass, and the money is gone from the investment accounts but not in my bank account. Now, the old me would have been freaking out and calling the bank to see what the heck was going on. How about you?

Instead, I prayed and asked: *God, Lord, do I need to call anyone? No.* Then, I had to ask the tough question: *Lord, will I get the money?* The reason this was tough to ask is because I had to be okay with His answer! Fortunately, the answer was yes, I was going to get the money, so I didn't stress.

A week went by, then two weeks, and again, money gone from the investment accounts, still not in my bank account. Three weeks go by. How would you be? Again, this was a substantial sum of money, more than the average American family makes in two to three years.

Three weeks and one day after I was supposed to get the money, the advisor emailed me and told me they needed a verbal 'okay' to release the funds, and it was released.

God loves me so much that instead of just receiving the money and not growing, He gave me the money and a massive upgrade with peace and patience.

We want the result, but results don't last.

Lessons will, though.

Questions and Prayers for Chapter 6...

Questions:

1. Where might God be attempting to grow you in peace and patience?

2. How has this chapter challenged the way you view money?

Prayer:

Father, thank You for being with me. Thank You for helping me view money as a resource and You as my source, Lord. Thank You for helping me to use money and not have money use me. I love You, and thank You in Jesus' name, Amen!

You must let your emotions go and not be addicted to whatever answer He is going to give you.

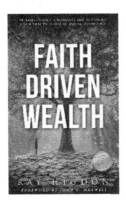

(Take a picture of this page, use #FaithDrivenWealth and post it to your favorite social media sites.)

7

GOD HAS AN ANOINTED BRAND FOR YOU

You heard that right. You have an anointed brand. What do I mean by that? It's basically a calling that's both authentic to you and divinely aligned. It's not just some slick packaging of a "marketable" skill but purpose-filled, and spirit-led. In the last year of working with clients, I came to realize that everyone has a calling that, *if* they pursue, would:

1. Help a lot of people, and...
2. Help them make more money and perhaps even grow in public recognition and status.

Do you know *you* have a calling? I bet you do, but you may not have it figured out yet.

One of my mentoring programs is called the Sales and Marketing Mentorship, and often, these group coaching calls go over a few hours as I work with students on discovering their anointed brand, help them overcome any sabotage (spiritual or mental), and also lay out strategies for them to execute for their brand.

How do you find your anointed brand?

The majority of the time, your anointed brand and who you are called to help is based on something you have overcome in life or actually **will** overcome.

Here are some examples I have given to students:

- Helping others forgive their mothers and fathers
- Helping people who hate church grow closer to God
- Helping parents reconcile with their adult children
- Helping a husband or wife forgive a spouse who cheated
- How to live your life with a non-curable health issue

What I don't do is come up with some cutesy, clever-sounding tagline or brand that sounds good. We collaborate and pray until we get the actual anointed brand that God is calling them to. At the end of this chapter, I will give you a few questions that could help you figure out your anointed brand.

Help the Person You Used to Be

People are seeking authorities more than experts. What's the difference? An expert has a degree, certificate, or some form of credential in the problem you are struggling with. An authority is someone who has been in your shoes.

If you were someone who has unfortunately dealt with the loss of a child, who would you rather talk to? A certified grief expert? Or another human who has dealt with the loss of *their* child? Most would pick someone who has been in their shoes, not the expert.

What Was Meant for Evil, God Can Use for Good

Everything we have gone through that was tough only makes sense if we stop looking at the hurt as hurt and instead look at what happened as a way to help others.

I don't regret any of the abuse I went through as a kid, as it helped me better connect and relate with kids and adults who have been through abuse. Pain is a connector if you can look outward (who can I help?) versus inward (how unfair it was to you). Then, you can turn your pain into purpose and step into a calling that will be the most fulfilling thing you can do as a career.

Often, the issue that we spend the most time working on now or in the past *is* God's anointed brand for us.

Why?

We are best equipped to help people with the things that we struggled with the longest and that were the toughest things we ever overcame. By the way, the concept of *your mess becoming your message* is biblical.

Judges 3:1-2 tells us that the Lord allowed some Israelites to experience war so they could prepare those who had yet to experience war.

You fought battles and a war that didn't break you but made you stronger. I believe the harder challenges you have gone through, the higher calling God has for your life.

How To Figure Out Your Anointed Brand

Of all the entrepreneurs, network marketers, authors, and speakers I have worked with, very few knew their actual anointed brand. Most were operating with a good-sounding brand that, to some degree or not, had worked but was *not* their actual *anointed* brand.

I used to think that your anointed brand had to be based on something you overcame, but I've learned that this is not the case. I estimate that around 85% of people have an anointed brand based on what they have been through. The other 15% fall into a couple of other categories.

Regarding the other 15%, and honestly, I hesitated to include this because more people will believe they fall into this category than is true. That said, there are some people called to a very specific value in the marketplace that may not be focused on what they have been through. Usually, these people have also been through a lot, but they have a special anointing for a particular space in the market that is not centered around their trauma.

Assuming you are in the majority that is called to serve the person you used to be, and want to figure out what that looks like, pray about the major things you have been through. Don't be surprised if it ends up being the one thing you most don't want to talk about!

I am grateful that I've now helped hundreds of clients with their anointed brand, and when they walk in that brand, magic happens. They see God's favor in all this walk, and doors fling wide open that were sealed tight prior.

For you to accept this, you must stop looking inward and look outward. You must stop looking at how unjust life has been and instead see all the people you are called to help. Focus on who you are anointed to help, and your life will become a much more fulfilling experience.

Questions and Prayers for Chapter 7...

Questions:

1. Make a list of the things you have been through (childhood, teen years, and as an adult) and pray about the list and thank God for revealing where He is calling you to walk. Father, what is my anointed brand?

2. Once armed with your anointed brand, ask yourself, how will it feel to start helping people who have gone through or are going through what you have been through?

Prayer:

Father, thank You for loving me and revealing to me my anointed brand. Thank You for equipping me to help so many people, Lord. You are worthy of my praise, and I am honored to be Your child. I thank You in Jesus' name. Amen!

Often, the issue that we spend the most time working on now or in the past is the anointed brand God has for us.

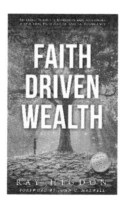

(Take a picture of this page, use #FaithDrivenWealth and post it to your favorite social media sites.)

8

THE ULTIMATE WEALTH HACK

I imagine many people who read this book will want to learn how to get wealthy. They've tried praying and praying for money to come in but have not seen that happen yet.

If that is you, it's likely you bounce from beating yourself up because you must be praying wrong to feeling like God isn't fair to you; He just doesn't care or love you.

The truth is He loves you so much, but He also wants you to grow into who you are called to be and how He sees you.

At the time of this writing, I have a 9-year-old daughter. If my daughter asked me for a Ferrari, I would *not* get her one, would you? Why not? She's not ready for it. She would not be able to handle it. It would be way overkill for where she is in life, and, of course, she is not old enough to drive it anyway.

Does this mean that I don't love her? Or does it mean I am selfish? Or that she's not good enough? None of those. She just isn't ready for it.

You need to hear this. It's a good chance that you also aren't ready for wealth. However, in <u>this</u> chapter, you will learn how to fix that.

How to Pray

Psalm 100:4 (NIV) says: *"Enter his gates with thanksgiving and his courts with praise..."*

Mark 11:24 (NIV) says, *"Whatever you ask for in prayer, believe that you have received it, and it will be yours."*

Philippians 4:6 (NIV) says, *"Do not be anxious about anything, but in every situation, by prayer and petition, with thanksgiving, present your requests to God."*

Notice in Philippians that it says "with thanksgiving" to present your requests to God. All of these point to a blueprint, and that blueprint, or "hack," is to thank God for what you want. However, I have learned that thanking Him for the traits you desire is much more fruitful than thanking Him for the results you want.

- A weak and non-biblical prayer would be, *Father, please bring me money.*

- A better but still not as powerful prayer would be, *Father, thank You for being my provider and bringing me more money.*

- The best prayer around this would be, *Father, thank You for being my provider and thank You for growing me in the wisdom to be able to steward larger amounts of money.*

Traits and lessons last, results don't. When you pray for a result, you are asking for a fleeting thing. You risk having the money stay your source and what you are attempting to derive all your fulfillment from, *which will never actually work.*

The ultimate wealth, and quite frankly, **life hack,** is to be in Thanksgiving, or gratitude, toward any trait you want. I do this all the time. I notice a trait I want or discover a trait in the Bible, and I just thank the Father for helping me develop that trait. And He does.

Now, if money is tight and you are upset, observe that money controls you. We cannot tell if money has a hold over us through our thoughts or language. We know it has control over us by observing our emotions. I hear people say all the time, "I trust God, but this money situation has me really stressed out. I don't know what to do." That is not trusting God. That is trusting money.

Find and Cherish the Lesson

Something doesn't go your way? Good! God is giving you a lesson that will last longer than just a result. All you must do is turn to Him and thank Him for growing you. Something fun that I do when I get something that would be perceived as bad news is I either thank Him for protecting me from something I didn't see, or I say, Lord, can't wait to see what You do with this!

Again, lessons last; results don't. If you don't get the lesson, that's actually okay; it will just be repeated. God loves you so much that He will repeat the lesson *until* you learn it.

Pay close attention to any patterns in your life. Regarding money, this often looks like you getting to a certain amount of money in earnings or savings, and then something going wrong. I assure you, there is a lesson there, and if you want to get off that roller coaster, turn to Him and thank Him for giving you the lesson He's been trying to help you with.

Questions and Prayers for Chapter 8...

Questions:

1. What have been any patterns with you and money? Think hard about this and get it repaired with His help.
2. What traits would you need to grow in to steward the amount of money and wealth you desire? Write them all down and then thank the Father for helping you grow in all of them.

Prayer:

Father, thank You for making me a better steward of money and resources. Thank You for growing me into the type of person who can and should have more money. And Father, thank You for helping me trust in You more than what is in my bank account. I thank You in the mighty name of Jesus Christ! Amen!

People say, "I trust God, but this money situation has me really stressed out. I don't know what to do!"

That is NOT trusting God. That is trusting money.

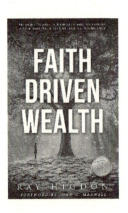

(Take a picture of this page, use #FaithDrivenWealth and post it to your favorite social media sites.)

A RADICAL TAKE ON GENEROSITY

There are two primary problems with how people think about generosity.

One, they give too much due to their aversion to wealth and their own self-worth issues.

Two, they give only to be recognized by others.

Matthew 6:1-4 (NIV) says: *"Be careful not to practice your righteousness in front of others to be seen by them. If you do, you will have no reward from your Father in heaven. So when you give to the needy, do not announce it with trumpets, as the hypocrites do in the synagogues and on the streets, to be honored by others. Truly I tell you, they have received their reward in full. But when you give to the needy, do not let your left hand know what your right hand is doing, so that your giving may be in secret. Then your Father, who sees what is done in secret, will reward you."*

So, we aren't to be generous to show off to someone or because we have some level of guilt, but to honor our Father as He sees all that we do.

I believe if God is calling you to a large level of wealth, He is going to have you learn to stop trusting in money and to trust Him. How will He do that? He will have you make uncomfortable decisions with your money.

He's had me invest in coaching when we faced too many expenses. He's had me give money to different charities in amounts that were way too much for where we were financially, keep those amounts secret, and give anonymously. He's had me write larger checks than what was currently in the bank account, only to show off and have the money *I needed to be there the next day!*

Now, this is not to encourage you to be reckless with money or to think that you can just write any check, and He will provide (I can't make those promises!) But the key in all these scenarios is that He nudged me to do these things. I prayed on them and got confirmation He wanted me to, so I did. Don't just think He will cover anything you write or any expense you get. His nature is to grow you, and if you need a lesson before He provides, He will take that opportunity to grow you.

Although the Bible does say in 2 Corinthians 9:6-13 that if you are generous, He will provide and have you be abundant in every way, I am not generous for that reason. I am generous because, quite frankly, all of my results, life, and money are His anyway, and I am just stewarding what He has given me. I never know why He tells me to give to one charity and not another or to help one friend and not another, but I know His ways are higher than my ways, and I trust Him.

I am generous, but not for the purpose of pleasing others, looking good, or getting some type of return. I am generous because He has been so generous with me.

In the past, I have agreed with the idea of setting aside 10% of what you make into a giving account and allocating that to be given away. Now that I have grown some, I no longer agree with that, as it doesn't take any faith to give what you have already saved up. I ask God every day if there's someone He wants me to bless or some organization He wants me to give to. I am the steward, not the driver or owner. By now, you, too, should be able to hear from Him.

If you are still struggling to hear His voice, shoot me a message on Facebook (Fb.com/rayhigdonpage) or Instagram @rayhigdon, and I will be happy to walk you through a 3-step process to hear His voice better.

Questions and Prayers for Chapter 9...

Questions:

1. Can you accept the idea that if you give without seeking praise from others, your heavenly Father will reward you?

2. Have you ever felt nudged to make a radical move with your money, but talked yourself out of it? Might that be a time when God wanted you to walk in faith?

Prayer:

Father, thank You for helping me discern when to give, how much, and to whom. Thank You for helping me have a giving heart that seeks You more than the praise of others. Thank You for helping me walk in faith regarding all aspects of money. I thank You in Jesus' name, Amen!

The ultimate wealth—and quite frankly, life hack—is to be in Thanksgiving or gratitude.

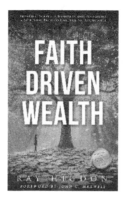

(Take a picture of this page, use #FaithDrivenWealth and post it to your favorite social media sites.)

10

TRUSTING IN GOD'S PLAN

Here's what I know: when God is calling you, He does *not* want you to trust in uncertain people *or* uncertain riches. When I turned to God, He revealed to me people in my life whom I thought loved me and whom I could count on, and He revealed their true character to me.

Proverbs 29:25 (NIV) points to the power and peace of placing your trust in God rather than in people: *"Fear of man will prove to be a snare, but whoever trusts in the Lord is kept safe."* This verse warns against living in fear of others' opinions, judgments, or approval because doing so is a trap that can limit you, compromise your integrity, or steer you away from your purpose. Simply put, the fear of human opinion disables, trusting in God protects you from that.

When it comes to money, I have seen it with client after client. God wants to take them away from trusting money and move them to truly trust in Him. This does NOT mean He wants you to be broke. As earthly mothers and fathers, we don't want to see our kids struggle, and He is perfect and certainly wants to see us thrive. But as I have said all throughout this book, He wants you to be dependent on Him, not money. I have seen those that were trusting in money go through a "refinding" period where money literally flies away from them. This is a clearing season, not a lifelong sentence. If you happen to be in a season where money is flying away from you faster than you are bringing it in, pray and see if this is God wanting you to rely on and draw closer to Him.

My mentor Graham Cooke says that nothing that starts in a negative can end in a positive. *When*, not *if*, you get a crushing blow, avoid starting with a negative, *"Oh, no!"* fear-based reaction. You want to instead react with, *"Oh boy, Lord, can't wait to see what You do with this!"*

Remember, whenever you are afraid, having anxiety or stress is when you aren't trusting Him. He is with you. He will never leave or forsake you, and you can do all things with Him.

Know that He is with you in every situation. No situation is a surprise to Him. He wants you to know you can trust Him, and we get to see that we can trust Him in situations that we don't know how to handle on our own.

All Provision Comes from God

No matter how much we grind or strategize, all provision comes from God. John 3:27 (NIV) tells us: *"A person can receive only what is given them from heaven."*

Think of it like this: you might be putting in work, but God's the one supplying the opportunities, the connections, and the resources. Everything you have is a blessing from Him. That steady paycheck, the unexpected bonus, the side hustle taking off, it's all God's way of showing up for you. And here's the kicker: God's supply never runs out.

So, while you might be focused on filling your bank account, don't forget to acknowledge the source. He's providing more than just financial stuff, too—He's giving you peace, joy, and security. When you remember that God is your ultimate provider, it takes the pressure off. You don't have to do it all on your own. God's got resources beyond what you can see. Let go of the stress and trust that He's got you covered, no matter what.

God is the source of your wealth. Your job, your investments, and even your entrepreneurial spirit come from Him. It's easy to get caught up in thinking you earned everything by your own hard work. Sure, you've put in the effort, but God's the one who blessed you with the opportunities and abilities to make things happen. When you recognize God as the source, it changes the game. You stop freaking out over every little financial dip and start trusting that He's got more than enough to keep you afloat. Your wealth isn't just about what's in your bank account—it's the peace, security, and opportunities God provides. So, next time you feel anxious or worried about money, take a step back and give God some credit. He's the real MVP when it comes to your success.

As it says in Proverbs 3:5-6 (NIV), *"Trust in the Lord with all your heart and lean not on your own understanding; in all your ways submit to him, and he will make your paths straight."*

One of the hardest lessons to learn is that God's timing isn't always in sync with our own. You might be ready to cash in on those blessings right now, but God often has other plans. Developing patience means trusting that God will bring abundance into your life at the perfect time, not a moment too soon or too late. Romans 8:25 (NIV) says, *"But if we hope for what we do not yet have, we wait for it patiently."*

In a world that's all about instant gratification, waiting can feel like a struggle. But here's the truth: waiting on God teaches you faith, perseverance, and trust. It's during the waiting periods that you grow the most. Just like a seed takes time to grow after being planted, so does the abundance God has in store for you.

Patience isn't passive, though. It's an active trust in God's plan. It's doing your part, staying faithful, and believing that He will come through. Abundance on God's timetable may not look like what you had in mind, but it will always exceed your expectations.

Trust in divine timing and keep the faith. Don't rush the process. God has got your back, and His plan for your life is better than anything you could imagine.

Your financial journey is just that. It's a journey. There will be highs, lows, and everything in between, but trust that God has a purpose for each phase. Whether you're in a season of abundance or scraping by, God's got lessons and growth for you in every part of the process. Maybe He's teaching you to trust Him more when things are tight, or maybe He's showing you how to manage wealth with wisdom when you're flourishing.

Whatever phase you're in, it's all part of a bigger picture that God's painting. Trust that He's leading you somewhere good, and each step, no matter how small or difficult, has a purpose.

Stay faithful, keep pushing, and know that God's got a plan for your financial journey—every part of it.

Creating Wealth through Unwavering Faith

When it comes to creating wealth, unwavering faith is your superpower. In the world of faith driven wealth, faith isn't just a belief; it's the fuel that drives everything.

Hebrews 11:1 (KJV) reminds us, *"Now faith is the substance of things hoped for, the evidence of things not seen."* This isn't about wishful thinking; it's a deep, unshakeable belief that God will provide, even when the path isn't clear.

Faith driven wealth starts with trusting that God wants the best for you. Jeremiah 29:11 (NIV) says, *"For I know the plans I have for you, plans to prosper you and not to harm you, plans to give you hope and a future."*

This promise from God should be at the core of your financial mindset. You must believe that abundance is not just possible but is already on its way to you. When you operate from a place of unwavering faith, you're aligning yourself with God's will and opening the door for His blessings to flow into your life.

But here's the deal—faith isn't passive. It requires action. James 2:26 (KJV) states, *"Faith without works is dead."* To create wealth, you need to back up your faith with steps that align with your vision. When you give out of love and obedience to God, you align yourself with His heart. You're saying, "God, I trust You with my resources, and I know You'll provide for me." This kind of faith-driven giving opens the door for God to pour out His blessings on you.

Questions and Prayers for Chapter 10...

Questions:

1. What area or areas of your life do you need to trust God in right now?

2. Do you understand that God is bigger than that area of concern you have? Health, money, relationships, etc.

Prayer:

Father, thank You for helping me trust You. Father, I turn my stress and fear to You, thank You for taking them from me. Father, I thank You for helping me to realize You are with me always and will never leave me. I love You, in Jesus' name. Amen!

FAITH DRIVEN WEALTH

No matter how much we grind or strategize, all provision comes from God.

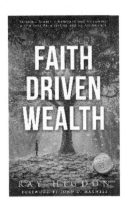

(Take a picture of this page, use #FaithDrivenWealth and post it to your favorite social media sites.)

11

TO GET WEALTHY, DO THIS

Now that we have covered so many things around wealth, sabotage, mindset, prayers, etc., let's talk about how to actually get wealthy.

You will get wealthy and have an abundant life when you:

- Understand God is the source and the creator of all results (John 3:27)
- Serve others. Make them, not you, first. Help others solve their problems and attain their desires.

That's it! What I find with those who are struggling financially is that they make their problems and woes first, and they don't trust God or believe He is the creator of their results.

At this point, I feel we've talked plenty about God being the creator of results, so hopefully, this book has already helped you with that part. Let's point out some things about making others first.

Are You Making Others First?

Anytime you stress, talk, or focus on *your* problems, you are focused inward, making yourself first, not others. It requires absolute diligence to avoid doing this. It is easy to fall into *what's wrong* versus *who I can serve*. It's normal to dwell on your problems versus the problems and goals of others. It's quite worldly to see your issues more vividly and emotionally than it is to recognize who you can serve.

Now, if you did the work in the chapter on your anointed brand, this *will* become easier. You can learn to catch yourself. 2 Corinthians 10:5 (NIV) says: *"We take captive every thought to make it obedient to Christ."* Another word for Christ is the Word of God. So, you examine your thoughts and determine if those thoughts are biblical. If they are not, you make them obedient to the Word of God. Let me help you with how to do that.

Speak to Yourself More Than You Listen to Yourself

Here are some common thoughts of those who constantly put themselves first *and* their biblical counterpart to exchange those self-serving thoughts:

I can't do it (or I am afraid):

- Philippians 4:13 (NKJV): *"I can do all things through Christ who strengthens me."*

I am stressed:

- Psalm 16:8 (NIV): *"With him at my right hand, I will not be shaken."*

I'm not worthy:

- Romans 8:16 (NIV): *"The Spirit himself testifies with our spirit that we are God's children."*

Money is bad:

- Psalm 35:27 (KJV): *"The Lord delights in the prosperity of his servant."*

I am worried/anxious about money:

- 1 Timothy 6:17 (NIV): *"...not to put their hope in wealth, which is so uncertain, but to put their hope in God..."*

I am confused or overwhelmed:

- Proverbs 3:5 (NIV): *"Trust in the Lord with all your heart and lean not on your own understanding."*

The more you catch your thoughts and exchange them for their biblical counterparts, the easier you will transition to having fewer and fewer of the selfish, inward-facing thoughts.

Now, I must say this: none of this is to get you to beat yourself up, as I know that is most likely your tendency. My goal is *zero* condemnation! Every Christian knows the verse from Romans 8:1 that there is no condemnation in Christ, yet His followers are riddled with self-condemnation. When you point this out, they typically beat themselves up for having ever condemned themselves.

Brothers and sisters, we must be smarter and stronger than this. When I say stop bashing yourself, that doesn't mean to just continue in some other way, it means to **stop it!**

When you beat yourself up, no one gets help from you, you don't shine the light of Christ, and you continue to dwell on the bad habits of being someone you are not, instead of a wonderful and loved Child of the Most High.

Now, watch your language around this and all things. Proverbs 18:21 tells us that life and death are in the power of the tongue. If you take any concept from this book and say something like, "That is going to be hard," then it will be. But, if instead you say, *"I can do all things through Christ who strengthens me,"* for anything you may feel would be hard, it will be easier.

Remember the chapter on the ultimate wealth hack? Well, remember that hack works for *any* trait you want to grow into.

Questions and Prayer for Chapter 11...

Questions:

1. What might be a "go-to" activity you choose to focus on any time you catch yourself focusing on your problems?

2. What verse do you resonate with that would be perfect as an exchange when you are thinking negatively?

Prayer:

Father, thank You for helping me catch my negative thoughts and quickly replace them with Your Word. Father, thank You for helping me realize that the world does not benefit from me beating myself up. Father, thank You for helping me to see myself the way You see me, Lord. I thank You in Jesus' name! Amen.

FAITH DRIVEN WEALTH

When you beat yourself up, no one gets help from you. You don't shine the light of Christ.

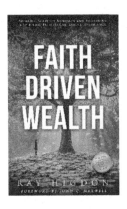

(Take a picture of this page, use #FaithDrivenWealth and post it to your favorite social media sites.)

12

THE BEST TYPE OF FREEDOM

The best type of freedom isn't financial. The best type of freedom is understanding that if you accept Christ, He is with you and abides in you as you abide in Him. The entire chapter of 1 John 4 does a beautiful job explaining this, but this verse in particular:

> *"If anyone acknowledges that Jesus is the Son of God, God lives in them and they in God."*
> **-1 John 4:15 (NIV)**

Five Biblical Truths About You

Here are five biblical truths that created a whole level of freedom for me that I never got from money, even when I became financially free:

1. Whatever was meant for evil, God will use for good.
2. I am a new creation; the old has passed away.
3. Jesus and the Holy Spirit are with me always.
4. I can do all things through Christ, who strengthens me.

5. God works for the good of those who love Him, who have been called according to His purpose.

Two Facts Often Forgotten
1. God did not give us a spirit of fear. Fear is never from God. Fear is either from our own mind or from the enemy. Any area of your life where you are afraid is where you are misaligned with God and are forgetting the five biblical truths I mentioned above.
2. There is no condemnation in Christ. Most Christians know this verse from Romans 8:1, but don't live it. They love dwelling on the idea of condemning themselves and their "not-enoughness."

What Does This Look Like?

I want to give you examples of what this looks like, or this will be just more head knowledge you think you know instead of applying.

Here are three examples of true freedom I have experienced:

- When I got a subpoena around an investment I was involved in, my reaction was, "Lord, I can't wait to see what You do with this."
- When we were in Israel on the day of the major attack on October 7th, 2023 (which I talked about in *The Faith Driven Network Marketer*), I knew we would be okay.
- When a neighbor confronted me because my dog accidentally peed on his son's lemonade stand sign, I

knew the Lord was about to create a new relationship for us.

I no longer experience stress, anxiety, or fear, as I know I'm with God and God is with me. Although I rarely experience any type of trigger or offense now, if that happens, I know it is only a gateway for transformation.

This way of being free is what makes sense of some otherwise strange verses in the bible, such as:

> *"Consider it pure joy, my brothers and sisters, whenever you face trials of many kinds, because you know that the testing of your faith produces perseverance. Let perseverance finish its work so that you may be mature and complete, not lacking anything."*
> **-James 1:2-4 (NIV)**

And...

> *"Not only so, but we also glory in our sufferings, because we know that suffering produces perseverance; perseverance, character; and character, hope."*
> **-Romans 5:3-4 (NIV)**

I have met many who are financially free. I don't believe any of them are stress-free. Consider a few examples from famous and successful people:

- After Markus Persson sold the popular game Minecraft and netted 1.75 billion he talked about how depressed and lonely he became.
- In a "60 Minutes" interview after winning his third Super Bowl, Tom Brady said most days he wondered if this was all there was to life.
- Jake Kassan sold his watch company to Movado at 27 and made $100 million. He said he always thought his purpose was to make money, but after making more than he ever imagined, he said it led him to depression.
- Loom founder Viney Hiremath sold his company for $975 million, only to also find himself lost and depressed.

Guess what? You can have both. So, regardless of where you are financially right now, you can enjoy what you perceive money will bring you: freedom from stress, anxiety, and fear.

Questions and Prayer for Chapter 12...

Questions:

1. What areas of my life are **not** worry, stress, or fear free? Where can you learn to trust God and that He's *got you* in those areas?

2. What would life look like if no one could cause you stress?

Prayer:

Father, thank You for helping me cast all my anxiety on You, as I know You care for me. Father, thank You for helping me identify any area of my life that isn't free and turning it over to You. Thank You for helping me with this in the mighty name of Jesus Christ, Amen!

Fear is never from God. Fear is either from our own mind or from the enemy.

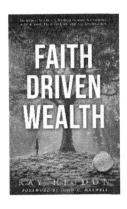

(Take a picture of this page, use #FaithDrivenWealth and post it to your favorite social media sites.)

NOTHING IS IMPOSSIBLE
(Guest Chapter by Tyler Watson)

When Jesus was talking about a rich person entering heaven, He said that with man, it is impossible, but with God, all things are possible.

For this chapter, I want you to hear from one of my good friends, Tyler Watson. Tyler is a world-changer and someone who has spoken multiple times at our *Faith Over Fear* event, and I appreciate his contribution to this book. I'm sure you will, as well.

From Tyler:

Nothing is impossible to those who believe.

That has been one of the guiding principles of my life and the reason I'm so excited to share this chapter with you.

No matter what is going on in your life right now, no matter what challenges you currently face or will face in your life, you have the ability to transform them into something incredible. I know that this is true.

Over the past decade, I've had the privilege of working with thousands of amazing people from all walks of life. I've helped stay-at-home moms and nine-figure entrepreneurs, influencers with millions of followers, and teenagers struggling with addiction. I've seen athletes break through to the next level, marriages go from the brink of divorce to blissful companionship, and business owners make in a day what used to take them a year.

In my work, so-called "impossible" things happen every day.

It wasn't always this way, however.

My Life Journey

My journey really began when I was 12 years old, and my world was shattered by my parents' divorce. Suddenly, everything felt impossible. I fell into addictions, suicidal thoughts, and putting on a face for everyone so that no one knew how broken I felt inside.

I spent years feeling like it was my fault, and no matter how hard I tried, I could never create the happy life I wanted for myself or my family. I was stuck on a racetrack with four flat tires, unable to stop or get off, but always running into things and causing myself and others pain while I used every ounce of energy I had to drive in an endless circle to nowhere.

Maybe you're struggling or have struggled with similar feelings.

You want so badly to change, but when you try, you end up making things worse or causing a problem in a different area of your life. You grow your business, but your marriage falls apart. You help your kids, but your body burns out. You finally pay attention to your health, but your profits start dropping.

And yet, there are people out there who seem to be able to make money, have relationships, and enjoy health and abundance. It appears that they are able to have it all.

Why?

At this point, I'm not going to start spouting some cliche advice about the law of attraction or hustle culture or your ability to think and grow rich.

But I am going to peel back the curtain a little bit about why my clients are able to see tangible shifts in just about every area of their lives in record time. The impossible becomes possible not just by casual, run-of-the-mill "thoughts" but through powerful beliefs directed in a specific way.

I Call It Alignment

I call it alignment, and it starts in the body, not the mind.

The truth is that nearly every result in this life comes from physical push and pull reactions in the body. Some people call this the "subconscious mind," but to me, it's nothing more than chemistry.

From the time we are babies, our physical being goes through experiences and forms 'push' responses (I call them allergies) and 'pull' responses (I call them addictions) not just to food or other substances, but to ideas and situations, such as 'money,' 'love,' and 'struggle.'

These physical reactions can be measured and directly influence our ability to have money, experience love, and break free from struggle. Everything we want in life but don't yet have, and everything we have but wish we didn't, can be traced back to these allergies and addictions.

We Are Here to Act

It is my personal belief that God sent us here to this planet to act, not to be acted upon. Our soul or essence has the ability to influence and ultimately change our body, not the other way around.

I also believe that we were each given a lesson to learn and a mission to accomplish in this life. That being the case, the purpose of nearly everything I do is to help people learn to shift the chemical reactions in the body so their soul can create what it is here to create.

Many people talk about faith as something we need to succeed. Faith in ourselves, those around us, and especially in God. I could write an entire book about faith and how I believe that it works. For now, though, I'd like to briefly touch on faith as it relates to what we've been discussing.

One of my favorite definitions of faith is a hope for something that isn't yet seen but is true. It's hard to have faith, for instance, that one day, the moon will literally turn into actual cheese because it simply isn't true and never will be. Not sure who would want that anyway, lol.

However, I believe that the things God has put in our hearts to accomplish in this life are actually "true" because they are already in us. We just need to bring them out of what is unseen to what is seen. That, to me, is faith.

The challenge comes because we live in a mortal world and, especially, a mortal body. When we seek to act in faith, with our belief in God and His purpose for us, our ability to believe and see our potential is tainted. We see things not according to the truth but according to our own allergies and addictions.

When we take action toward our goals, our old patterns show up and create chaos in our lives. One area of success creates another one of failure because that is simply what our body is used to. We are addicted to fear, worry, and anger, so when it looks like we are becoming free, we end up sabotaging ourselves. We binge eat. We get into an argument. Flub the sale, wreck the car, etc., because of an addiction to what we *don't* want and an allergy to what we *do* want.

Alignment is a simple process I created to shift the chemical responses in the body and help you find freedom.

Remember that you are a powerful child of God, and everything is possible to you.

-Tyler Watson

To learn more, please visit: alignmenteffect.com/raybook

50 POWERFUL PRAYERS

Although the end of each chapter in this book contains a powerful prayer associated with the chapter contents, I wanted to create a chapter solely focused on some prayers that have helped me and will help you. This may become the chapter you come back to the most and I felt it was the perfect way to wrap up the book.

50 Powerful Prayers (as always, I suggest saying them out loud)

1. Father, thank You for helping me accept and understand You are the source of my wealth and provision.
2. Father, thank You for helping me embrace that You delight in my prosperity.
3. Father, thank You for helping me understand that I can prosper in all things and be in health, just as my soul prospers.
4. Father, thank You for helping me use the gifts You've given me to serve others.
5. Father, thank You for helping me understand that I am Your child and You love me.
6. Father, thank You for helping me see and accept You as my provider and mentor.

7. Father, thank You for helping me understand that I am wonderfully made in Your image.

8. Father, thank You for taking all my worries, anxiety, and fear.

9. Father, thank You for helping me trust You.

10. Father, thank You for helping me rely on and trust You.

11. Father, thank You for blessing the work of my hands.

12. Father, thank You for revealing any area where You want me to grow.

13. Father, thank You for helping me see myself the way You see me.

14. Father, thank You for helping me truly understand that You are with me and will never leave or forsake me.

15. Father, thank You for more than enough in all areas of my life.

16. Father, thank You for healing all parts of me.

17. Father, thank You for healing, harmony, order, and balance in all areas of my mind, body, and heart.

18. Father, thank You for your wisdom and discernment in all areas of my life.

19. Father, thank You for helping me bring more hope to others and more glory to You.

20. Father, thank You for enlightening me more and more each and every day.
21. Father, thank You for Your favor that goes before me.
22. Father, thank You for helping me believe I deserve all good things.
23. Father, thank You for making me excellent at receiving.
24. Father, thank You for helping me delight in being obedient to You.
25. Father, thank You for helping me know You love me.
26. Father, thank You for having my eyes see what You want me to see.
27. Father, thank You for helping me see my worth and value.
28. Father, thank You for protecting me and my family.
29. Father, thank You for blessing me and my family.
30. Father, thank You for giving me more energy in all my communications.
31. Father, thank You for helping me hear You better every day.
32. Father, thank You for helping me see my business as Your business.

33. Father, thank You for helping me have more honor and respect toward others.

34. Father, thank You for helping me have more trust and respect toward myself.

35. Father, thank You for helping me be happy from the inside out and the outside in.

36. Father, thank You for growing me in the fruit of the Spirit.

37. Father, thank You for growing my faith every day.

38. Father, thank You for healing my conscious and unconscious so I can better receive Your blessings and favor.

39. Father, thank You for helping me discern what You want me to stop doing.

40. Father, thank You for helping me trust You more than I trust money.

41. Father, thank You for increasing my desire to read Your Word.

42. Father, thank You for bringing me the perfect people and mentors to grow.

43. Father, thank You for bringing me someone today to help.

44. Father, thank You for helping me see that You chose me.

45. Father, thank You for increasing my creativity in my business and life.

46. Father, thank You for increasing all my relationships.

47. Father, thank You for helping me turn to You in every decision I need to make.

48. Father, thank You for helping me seek Your Kingdom first.

49. Father, thank You for revealing to me the secrets of Your Kingdom.

50. Father, thank You for restoring to me the joy of my salvation!

CONCLUSION

If you've made it to this point, *thank you*. I don't take that lightly. My hope is that something in these pages helped shift something for you. A belief, a burden, or a faulty assumption you've been carrying for years.

Writing *Faith Driven Wealth* wasn't just a project; it was an act of obedience. I've spent years chasing success, then redefining it. I've had money, lost it, made more, and learned what matters most. None of it compares to the peace, purpose, and partnership I've found in my relationship with God. He is the source of every result I've ever had, and every breakthrough I've ever experienced.

If you walk away with anything from this book, I pray it's this: you are not disqualified. God wants to bless you. He doesn't want you to struggle and also doesn't want you to make money your master, but He does want to bless you as His child. He's not looking for you to be perfect, but I believe He looks to us to be willing.

That said, wealth is a tool. Don't fear it, don't worship it, be a steward of it. Let your hands be open so He can flow it through you. And when the world tells you it's impossible, remember: God's economy is different. His timing is perfect. Thank you for letting me walk this journey with you. I believe the best is yet to come.

Love you,

Ray

FAITH DRIVEN WEALTH

About Ray Higdon

RAY HIGDON is the CEO of the Higdon Group; they help business owners increase their profits while putting God first. Since 2017, Ray has helped sales teams generate over 300,000 new customers and recruit over 70,000 new sales reps.

Ray has shared the stage with world-renowned thought leaders and business icons, including Tony Robbins, Robert Kiyosaki, Bob Proctor, Magic Johnson, Les Brown, Gary Vaynerchuk, and many more.

Ray's podcast, Home Business Profits, has over 10 million downloads.

His company, the Higdon Group, has been recognized as an Inc. 5000 company and hosts live and virtual events where thousands of people gain knowledge and sharpen their skills every year.

Ray is a dad to four wonderful kids and a proud husband to his wife, Jessica. They live in Naples, Florida.

Follow Ray on YouTube at HigdonGroup.com/channel. Ray blogs almost daily on **www.RayHigdon.com**

Increase Your Impact Grow Your Income

Would you like to increase your impact and your income?

My brand new company is a Kingdom Mentorship movement that includes events, gatherings, small groups and an app with over 600 transformational trainings!

This is something that you can even promote and earn by referring others.

Jump into our 5 day FREE trial today at: BrilliantMovement.com/movement

You Might Also Enjoy...

The Faith Driven Network Marketer

Navigating Your Path to Prosperity and Spiritual Fulfillment with God's Guidance.

In 2022, through a series of divinely timed meetings and conversations, Ray's future and life completely changed when he accepted Jesus Christ as his Lord and Savior.

In his most important work to date for the network marketing profession, Ray unveils his raw and riveting testament, sharing his lessons in network marketing and how they intersect with his newfound faith and the transformative impact it has had on every aspect of his life.

Discover the foundational principles that underpin Ray's faith-driven approach to network marketing. From obedience to stewardship, Ray's insights offer a roadmap for building a profitable business grounded in faith, integrity, and abundance.

For the network marketer who has found faith (or would like to), this book is the perfect marriage between getting you the results you seek while adhering to and following biblical teachings.

Ray shares specific prayers for each of these critical areas of focus. You'll also read about how Ray would rely on his faith alone when he and his wife Jessica found themselves on a holy trip that turned into an all-out war.

Available in paperback, ebook, and audiobook.

Made in United States
Orlando, FL
12 June 2025